Praise for 50 Tips for Terrific Teams

50 Tips for Terrific Teams is a treasure chest full of practical tools and wisdom for all team leaders and coaches. We will be drawing upon the practices, tips, and techniques contained in '50 Tips' to help and contribute to the teams in which we are participants, leaders and coaches. '50 Tips' is a great companion resource to the authors' **High Performance Team Coaching** *book.*

- Lillas Marie Hatala and **Richard Hatala**
Co-authors of *Integrative Leadership: Building a Foundation for Personal, Interpersonal, and Organizational Success*

I found reading **50 Tips for Terrific Teams** *to be more of a journey than a read because as I was walking through it, I was motivated to evaluate my team and where we were at. It is a good leadership guide in the way it is written because it is crisp in the research and leadership principles, not overdone. The addition of practical actions made it easy for me to apply the tips immediately to my new team.*

- Linda Dalgetty
Chief Information Officer, Agrium

I love it when someone comes up with a book that is concise, clear, incredibly useful, and easy to work with. We all live and work with other people, and we all need to get better at it. Here is a collection of great ideas that you can put to use almost any day in just about any organization. It is a great resource for anyone working with teams, and every leader and team member should have one on their desk. You can pick an idea to try this week, try another tip the week after, and keep harvesting new insights for months to come.

- Dr. Ric Durrant
CEC (Certified Executive Coach), PCC (Professional Certified Coach)
Leadership Specialist and Executive Coach

*While many leaders and coaches are well intentioned, they are frequently disappointed with their outcomes when trying to create high performing teams. **50 Tips for Terrific Teams** has brilliantly integrated the research (which few of us have time to sort through) and translated it into practical suggestions that will absolutely help create the desired shifts. This guide is user friendly and is the closest thing to having your own personal sage. I would recommend this book as an essential tool for anyone who leads a team or works with or on a team.*

- **Denise Still**, MSW, RSW PCC, CEC (Certified Executive Coach)
Manager Organization Development, Calgary Board of Education

50 Tips for Terrific Teams

Proven Strategies
for
Building High Performance Teams

Dr. Jacqueline Peters
and
Dr. Catherine Carr

InnerActive
LEADERSHIP ASSOCIATES INC.

Produced by:

FriesenPress
Suite 300 – 852 Fort Street
Victoria, BC, Canada V8W 1H8

www.friesenpress.com

Distributed to the trade by The Ingram Book Company

Also by

Dr. Jacqueline Peters and Dr. Catherine Carr

High Performance Team Coaching

A Comprehensive Approach for Leaders and Coaches

www.HighPerformanceTeamCoaching.com

Contents

Acknowledgments

Just when our families thought that the long hours of writing our doctoral dissertations were over, we decided to keep writing and turn our research into a couple of useful and easy-to-read books: *50 Tips for Terrific Teams* and *High Performance Team Coaching: A Comprehensive System for Leaders and Coaches*. We wrote *50 Tips for Terrific Teams* because we wanted a book that team leaders and professionals could pick up and quickly find helpful research based strategies for working with their teams more effectively.

We are grateful to those who shared this writing journey with us: the researchers whose work we quoted; our mentors, Peter Hawkins, Annette Fillery-Travis and David Lane; and the many friends, family, colleagues and clients who gave both candid and encouraging feedback on drafts of the book. Our thanks go to Judy Au, Jennifer Britton, Dr. Elaine Cox, Linda Dalgetty, Ric Durrant, Barb Francis, Lillas Marie Hatala, Richard Hatala, Colleen Lemire, Andrew Parsons, Joe Peters, Denise Still, Saida Vuk, and Janet Wannop.

We are so appreciative of our graphic designer, Andrea Lifton, who provided many great ideas and had an enthusiastic, collaborative, and patient approach to our many changes and requests. Thanks also to Lee Tunstall, our editor, for her wise counsel and speedy editing.

We also appreciate one another for our own terrific teamwork that included many early morning Skype calls filled with excitement and clarity, or pondering and puzzling over revisions sent back and forth, and quick learning about just what it takes to write and publish a book. We made it to the finish line together, feeling very grateful to have drawn on each other's talents and strengths. After all, that is what terrific teams are all about!

Jacqueline and Catherine

Foreword

Leadership in today's VUCA world (Volatile, Unpredictable, Complex and Ambiguous) requires high performing leadership teams, in which there is shared leadership and responsibility for addressing the fast changing challenges and ensuring the team and business perform at more than the sum of their parts. The old approach where the CEO was the only point of integration and the team was like a hub and spoke with team members each reporting in on their function is no longer fit for purpose. Yet I meet so many CEOs who need help in how to transition from the old style to the new shared leadership style necessary for becoming a high performing team.

There is so much good research and writing on high performing teams now (Hackman, 2012; Hawkins, 2011; Katzenbach and Smith, 1993; Wageman *et al.*, 2008 to name just some of the more well-known), but few CEOs have the time to access it. So how good to have this short, accessible and practical collection of tips on how to transform your team, by Catherine and Jacqueline, two very experienced team coaches who have both thoroughly researched all the best literature and found ways of applying it to teams across different sectors. They are both true "Pracacademics," that is practitioners whose practice is informed by deep research, and researchers and writers whose writing is informed and developed by their practical experience.

The journey from leading a "hub and spoke" team with oneself at the centre to a team of shared leadership and mutual responsibility, is a challenging but necessary journey for all of us who are leaders. We need all the support and help we can find and I certainly will be using a number of these tips to improve the boards I chair and the teams I lead. I hope you too find they aid you on your journey.

Peter Hawkins
Author of *Leadership Team Coaching* (Kogan Page, 2011)
Chairman of several companies and Team and Board Coach
Professor of Leadership Henley Business School

50 Tips for Terrific Teams

Proven Strategies
for
Building High Performance Teams

Introduction

Introduction

Terrific Teams
require effort, knowledge,
skills, and structure.

Teamwork is the ability to work together
toward a common vision.
The ability to direct individual accomplishments
toward organizational objectives.
It is the fuel that allows common people
to attain uncommon results.
- Andrew Carnegie

Almost everyone has had the misfortune of being on a terrible team. Poor design, miscommunication, conflict among teammates, and confusion over direction are some of the things that can keep a team from accomplishing its goals. On the other hand, a TERRIFIC team is a great experience! When things go right on a team, there is a synergy that allows the team to succeed in ways that are far greater than any one individual would ever be able to do alone. This synergy does not happen by chance, though. **Terrific Teams**, those that achieve high performance and engagement, have a combination of strong **effort, knowledge, skills and structure**.

Allow us to introduce ourselves. We are Jacqueline Peters and Catherine Carr and besides the many years of experience we've had in coaching teams and leading teams, we've done a lot of research on what makes teams terrific—and what makes them terrible (Carr and Peters, 2012). In this book, we have distilled and highlighted 50 key tips that we use in our own work with teams and leaders on a daily basis. By understanding the behaviours and actions that are most important and impactful for a team—and which ones aren't—you can make sure that your team is terrific!

Our years of experience working in organizations confirms for us that leaders are busy and don't have time to read and stay abreast of all the research that is out there – they have teams to lead and organizations to run! However, for those who are keen to read more on a particular topic, we have provided a full reference list at the end that highlights the key research that underpins the suggestions made throughout the book.

Some ideas for using these tips practically with your teams are:

▶ Read and reflect on the tips to evaluate your current team functioning and effectiveness.

▶ Choose a tip a week and review it at your team meeting. Have an open dialogue using the questions as a guide, or create your own. Create action plans to apply the tips in relevant and useful ways for your team.

▶ Plan a staff retreat. Ask staff to read the *50 Tips for Terrific Teams* book ahead of time. Pick three tips to discuss in depth and create action plans around those.

▶ Engage a coach or HR specialist to observe your team, assess your team effectiveness and provide feedback on strengths and gaps for your team to discuss. Select a few tips that further leverage your team's strengths or mitigate some weaknesses.

We also include the graphic summary of the High Performance Team Coaching (HPTC) system from our book titled *High Performance Team Coaching: A Comprehensive System for Leaders and Coaches*. We developed the HPTC system as a result of years of team coaching experience and our case study research on team coaching. Many of these 50 tips were inspired by and are part of this comprehensive approach to coaching business teams for leaders and professional coaches.

Now let's move on to the proven, research-based tips that you can use to accelerate the growth and development of your own terrific team!

High Performance Team Coaching System
© Peters and Carr, 2013

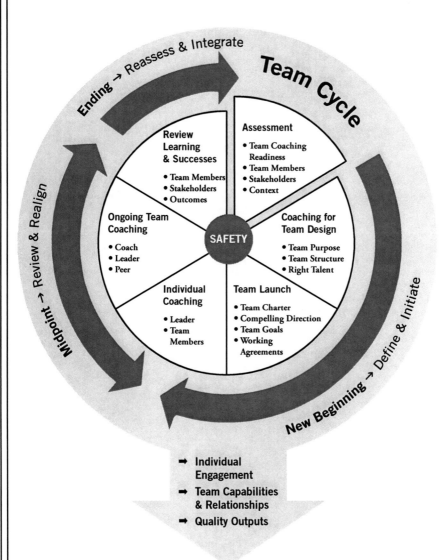

Team Cycle

Ending → Reassess & Integrate

Midpoint → Review & Realign

New Beginning → Define & Initiate

SAFETY

Review Learning & Successes
- Team Members
- Stakeholders
- Outcomes

Assessment
- Team Coaching Readiness
- Team Members
- Stakeholders
- Context

Ongoing Team Coaching
- Coach
- Leader
- Peer

Coaching for Team Design
- Team Purpose
- Team Structure
- Right Talent

Individual Coaching
- Leader
- Team Members

Team Launch
- Team Charter
- Compelling Direction
- Team Goals
- Working Agreements

➡ Individual Engagement
➡ Team Capabilities & Relationships
➡ Quality Outputs

Team Effectiveness

Team Design
and Structure

Tip #1

Learn what makes a team effective.

(Hint: Reading this book is a great start!)

Currently, many team interventions rely on incomplete approaches to supporting a team, and they use methods that "feel good but may not do good." In fact, some research indicates that despite being fun, most team-building events offer a minimal Return on Investment (ROI) (Wageman *et al.*, 2008). Many team interventions are based on face validity, not solid knowledge about what actually creates **team effectiveness** and long-term changes in performance. It is important for team leaders, coaches, and facilitators to learn some basics about team effectiveness, group process, and team coaching research so that their approaches can be as effective and productive as possible.

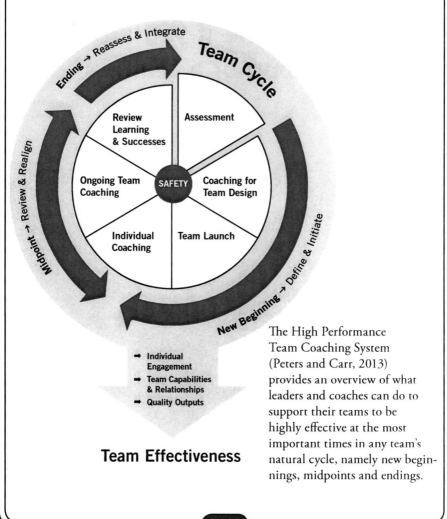

The High Performance Team Coaching System (Peters and Carr, 2013) provides an overview of what leaders and coaches can do to support their teams to be highly effective at the most important times in any team's natural cycle, namely new beginnings, midpoints and endings.

Tip #2

**Determine if you are
a group or a team.**

Individual commitment to a group effort—
that is what makes a team work, a company work,
a society work, a civilization work.
- Vince Lombardi, American Football Coach

A **real team** is defined as having clear boundaries, interdependent goals, and clarity of membership. In other words, knowing clearly who is on the team and who is not a regular team member is important (Wageman *et al.*, 2008).

It is also critical for the team to know when they need the support and input of all team members versus when they can work more independently. This does not mean that a team must do everything together or be interdependent to achieve all goals. However, there must be at least some interdependence and common objectives, or else the team is really just a group.

A group is a collection of individuals that have something in common but truly do not need to work together regularly to achieve their goals. They are also not rewarded for working together the way a real team is. Being a group is not a problem; it just means a different way of working.

ACTIONS

▶ To determine if you are more like a group or more like a team, ask:

- *What goals does the team have that truly require all of your team members to work together?*

- *Do all team members agree about who is on the team and who is not?*

- *How are your team members rewarded and/or compensated? Solely for meeting individual goals or for meeting at least some shared goals?*

▶ Ensure the team is interdependent, not just a group of people assigned to the same task or function. If you are more like a group, then make sure you collaborate but don't demand unnecessary interdependent teamwork.

Tip #3

Set the conditions for team success.

Success in business, as well as in life, is directly dependent
on the quality of the people you surround yourself with.
- Phil Hickey, CEO

Creating the **conditions** for team success is so critical that team structure and design alone accounts for 60 per cent of team effectiveness (Hackman, 2011). Front-end loading matters, so take the time to set things up well. No matter how great a house looks on the outside, any reputable contractor knows that what really counts is the structure—the quality of both the foundation and the materials. It is the same with a team.

Design the foundational structures well and put the right materials, or people in this case, in place first. Wageman *et al.* (2008) found that in the highest performing leadership teams there were six conditions for team effectiveness: three essential and three enabling conditions.

ACTIONS

▶ Make sure your team addresses the three essential conditions:

- You have a **real team** with clear membership and boundaries.

- There is a **compelling purpose** to guide the team's work.

- Your team has the **right people** with the knowledge, skills, and experience to perform the requisite work.

▶ Remember these three important enabling conditions as well:

- A **solid team structure** of less than 10 members who have a clear set of norms / agreements to guide how you can work together.

- A **supportive organizational context** that provides the information, time, and resources to be able to do your work.

- **Competent team coaching** from an internal or external coach, aimed at helping you and your team members grow individually and as a team.

Tip #4

Maximize effectiveness by having 10 members or less.

It is better to have one person working with you
than three people working for you.
- Dwight D. Eisenhower, 34th President of the United States

There has been hundreds of years of research on what the ideal team size is to optimize performance. Even as early as the 1800s, a French agricultural engineer named Maximilian Ringleman discovered that when more people pulled on a rope, each individual contributed less effort. He coined the term "social loafing" and many researchers since then have confirmed this phenomenon. So what is the right size for a team?

Wageman *et al.* (2008) suggest that a leadership team should be small, ideally having **six to eight members**. This size will allow the team to be optimally effective for decision making and getting their strategic work done.

Once the team exceeds 10 members, the leader will often spend more time trying to create a team that gels instead of effectively discussing and solving problems, or making decisions together. Large teams particularly suffer from this social loafing phenomenon in which a small handful of people do most of the work. Social loafing is especially common if each team member's accountabilities are not clear or enforced.

ACTIONS

▶ To determine if your team is the right size to be effective, ask:

- *How easy is it for your team to make decisions, include everyone, and use all the talent you have on the team?*

▶ If you have a larger team, consider breaking the team into smaller teams or subgroups, with only one of those groups having key accountability for the decision making and oversight of the broader team.

▶ If you are not able to change your team size or break into smaller teams, consider setting up subcommittees so everyone on the team has a task or focus that he or she feels inspired to contribute to and "own."

Tip #5

Create a strong team design and structure.

Effective team leaders take the time to properly **design** their team for success and set up the **structure** that will facilitate team effectiveness, before they focus on interpersonal dynamics and group processes (Hackman and O'Connor, 2005; Hackman and Wageman, 2005; Wageman *et al.*, 2008). As they set a compelling direction and purpose for their team, they also ensure that the right talent is in place. They define team structures such as roles and responsibilities, and they collaboratively identify working agreements that allow their team to deliver on their purpose and goals.

Addressing structure and design issues first will minimize conflict and confusion later and ultimately support the team to succeed.

ACTIONS

▶ To determine if you have a strong team design, ask your team members:

- *Do you clearly know what is expected of you and your other team members (roles and responsibilities)?*

- *Do you have a purpose and clear goals that actually require you to work interdependently to achieve them?*

- *Do you have explicit team norms and agreements about how to work together? Can you list what they are?*

- *Do you have the time, resources, and information it takes to get the job done properly?*

- *Do you have clear measures of success?*

▶ Use your own observations and feedback from your team on the questions above to design or redesign the team roles and structures to be as effective as possible.

Tip #6

Get real about the information, time, and resources your goals require.

A key condition for team success is making sure that your team actually has the **right resources** to be successful. This is one of the six conditions that Wageman *et al.* (2008) outline as a differentiator between high and low performing teams. The problem is that most teams are faced with limited time, money, and resources to deliver on their objectives and must fit within these constraints. So what does a team do? Try a reality check.

Ensure you and your team either advocate for the resources you need or have conversations to adjust stakeholder expectations to better meet the deliverables you can offer, given the resources you have.

ACTIONS

▸ Although this makes intuitive sense, be honest as a team and consider:

- *How effectively have you been advocating for the information, time and resources needed for your team to be successful?*

- *How have you been trying to accommodate and "make do" with best efforts?*

- *What is the level of frustration and feelings of being overwhelmed among team members as a result of insufficient time, resources, or information?*

- *How might the lack of resources ultimately sabotage your effectiveness?*

▸ Reduce the scope of deliverables if possible. Ensure that you review alternatives and actively negotiate and renegotiate the goals, outcomes and results required to best match the resources available to your team.

▸ Stay positive yet realistic if you are the team lead. Your role modelling will set the stage for how your team members feel about the team's goals and workload.

▸ If you lack confidence or have been unsuccessful in advocating for the resources you need, consult a trusted colleague or external coach. Ask them to help you create a plan for the difficult conversations needed with bosses, sponsors, and staff about appropriate expectations and deliverables.

Tip #7

Hold an effective team launch.

Team effectiveness researcher, Richard Hackman (2011), states that an effective **team launch** accounts for up to 30 per cent of team effectiveness. A team launch usually takes one or two days and is held away from the regular office environment to support the team to have uninterrupted interaction together. A facilitator or team coach from outside the team is often instrumental so that everyone can participate freely. Creating a safe team launch is critical to set the foundation for the team to be effective (Carr and Peters, 2012).

A team launch is the opportunity to step back, pull the team together, and plan the foundation to work together effectively. This includes both WHAT *and* HOW the work gets done. If the team is not brand new, re-launch it by creating a new focus, project, strategy, or goal for the team.

ACTIONS

▸ Make sure you agree upon these key elements during your one or two-day team launch:

- Guiding principles for your team, such as your vision, mission, and values.

  o **Vision** statements explain *WHY* your team or organization is doing the work and *WHERE* it is going in the future.

  o **Mission** statements tell *WHAT* your team does.

  o **Values** statements explain *HOW* your team will do that work.

- Clarity about the purpose of your team, key goals, roles and responsibilities, and working agreements or norms.

- Measures of success – identify at least two ways your team will know that it's more effective six, twelve, and eighteen months from now.

Tip #8

Create a Team Charter.

A **Team Charter** is a document that captures the team's vision, mission, values, purpose, goals, roles and responsibilities, working agreements, and success measures. The most effective teams take the time to create a clear team charter, especially if it is at the start of working together or at the time of a new beginning for the team (e.g., a new mandate, strategy, project, fiscal year, etc.). This investment will pay back dividends over time by providing a clear direction and decreasing miscommunications (Carr and Peters, 2012). Further, companies whose employees understand the mission and goals enjoy on average a 29 per cent greater financial return than other firms (Watson Wyatt Work Study, 2004).

ACTION

Ensure that you use the team charter as an active agreement that is reviewed and updated regularly and, when necessary, to guide how your team works effectively together. Too many such documents get filed, never to be seen again. We have found that the most useful charters can be summarized on one page like the team charter template below.

TEAM CHARTER for TEAM NAME DATE		
Vision		
Team Mission or Mandate or Purpose		
Team Members	**Working Agreements**	**Key Goals**
Values		**Success Measures**

Tip #9

Set norms and working agreements.

In the absence of rules, people make up their own.
- Blair Singer, Author and CEO

Working agreements are central to team success (Carr and Peters, 2012; Singer, 2004; Wageman *et al.*, 2008). Working agreements include the guiding principles, norms, or rules that teams agree upon about *HOW* they will support one another, run meetings, make decisions, communicate, and manage reporting. Richard Hackman (2012) suggests that a few essential principles, norms, and working agreements are enough to guide a group. Experiment with a few agreements to start and then review and revise the agreements over time.

ACTIONS

▶ To identify potential working agreements, ask your team members:

• *What issues repeatedly interfere with our team's performance?*

• *What enhances your own engagement and performance on the team?*

• *What behaviours shut you down?*

• *What key agreements need to be followed to reach our goals?*

▶ Discuss the consequences of *NOT* abiding by the working agreements.

▶ Some sample working agreements are:

• *We start and end meetings on time.*

• *We listen and ask questions to understand rather than judge what is said.*

• *We assume good intentions when differences or conflicts occur.*

• *We create an atmosphere of openness by focusing on the issue, not the person.*

▶ Follow up regularly on how your team is using the working agreements. A list of agreements on paper is only a list — you need to actively use and review them as a team to keep them relevant.

Tip #10

Refresh the team with a relaunch.

When it is obvious that the goals cannot be reached,
don't adjust the goals, adjust the action steps.
- Confucius

If the team was not launched properly when it was formed or if the team is at the beginning of a significant new team task or project, then **relaunch** the team. Also, if a team loses its momentum and things get stale, a **relaunch** can help to reset, refresh and refocus the team.

This relaunch tip is based on the finding that coaching interventions are best matched to times when coaching can make the most difference: the beginning, middle or end of a team's work (Gersick, 1988; Wageman *et al.*, 2009). Create a new beginning or conduct a midpoint review with the team to keep them aligned, engaged and productive.

ACTIONS

▶ You can find many ways to create a new beginning for an intact team, such as:

- Align around key, interdependent team objectives for the fiscal year.

- Roll out a new structure, mandate, or strategy.

- Leverage the arrival or departure of a team member to review and update the team charter if you have one, or create a team charter if you don't already have one.

▶ Once you refresh or relaunch your team, allow sufficient time to pass before attempting this again as teams may start to feel "change fatigue."

▶ After relaunching your team, share your new or revised team charter with other teams you work with regularly to foster productive cross-functional discussions and agreements. Clear understandings about roles, goals, working agreements, etc. can help break down barriers and silos that contribute to miscommunications between teams as much as within teams.

Tip #11

Address team dysfunction quickly.

Hackman (1976:1) says that groups:

... also have a shady side... They can, for example, waste the time and energy of members, rather than use them well. They can enforce norms of low rather than high productivity (Whyte, 1955). They sometimes make notoriously bad decisions (Janis, 1982). Patterns of destructive conflict can arise, both within and between groups (Alderfer, 1977) and groups can exploit, stress, and frustrate their members.

The lesson from this dark side quote is not to wait too long to address problems. If there are dysfunctional patterns at play, review and reconsider the team design and structure, and then address interpersonal dynamics that still do not improve. Once in motion, negative team dynamics can get stuck in place and become self-reinforcing (Fredrickson and Losada, 2005). This dark side can expand if not kept in check, and can become a toxic culture for a work group, a team, a department, or even an entire organization.

ACTIONS

▶ If you notice that some negative dynamics have become ingrained, identify the most disruptive behaviours and discuss the negative consequences with your team. Ask the team, *"How do we feel about how we are working together right now?"*

▶ As a team, identify what your desired future is and highlight the gap between the current and future state.

▶ Ask your team to identify the structures and behaviours that keep the negative patterns in place, and identify new structures, behaviours, and agreements that would support your desired future state.

▶ Invite an observer to attend one of your team meetings and share his or her observations. Objective feedback may help identify potential changes.

Team Players

Tip #12

Choose or develop the right players.

Getting the **right people** on the bus is a common refrain when building teams and it is not surprisingly a strong theme in the research on effective teams. This is described as "having the right people" in Hackman and Wageman's team effectiveness model (Wageman *et al.*, 2008), "having the right players" in Guttman's (2008) model, and having people with "adequate technical know-how" in LaFasto and Larson's (2001) model.

Many leaders will say, "That's great, but I am stuck with the people I have now and that's not changing any time soon. What do I do with who I've got?" Do an informal assessment of people, roles, and goals and hold some courageous conversations if needed.

ACTIONS

▶ Conduct a thorough knowledge and skills gap analysis, analyzing team member and whole team strengths and gaps in both technical skills and team skills. A spreadsheet can be a helpful tool for mapping this analysis.

▶ Hold challenging, honest individual conversations about the strengths and gaps each person has in his or her ability to meet your team's purpose and goals. Offer your feedback and ask how the team members see setting themselves up for success.

▶ Create a joint plan with individual team members to attend to any major gaps through training, coaching, mentorship, performance management, or role redefinition.

▶ If you find someone is clearly not a fit for the team, partner with the individual and others to explore different role options in the organization if at all possible. The longer you keep someone in a role that does not suit them well, the more painful it will be for you, them, and the team. It's not a gift to let someone gain a reputation for mediocrity, so try all avenues to create a win-win option.

Tip #13

Select women... and men with emotional and social intelligence.

Anita Woolley and a team of colleagues (2010) have studied the factors that enhance the **collective intelligence** of a team and identified some provocative findings. They observed that teams with more women on them are better at brainstorming, make better decisions, and solve problems more effectively. They are even more effective than teams that are made up of individuals who have higher IQs.

> *It's a preliminary finding—and not a conventional one. The standard argument is that diversity is good and you should have both men and women in a group. But so far, the data show, the more women, the better.* (Wooley and Malone, 2011:2)

Woolley and Malone surmised that women make better team members because they are often more socially sensitive and responsive to emotional cues than men typically are. In the end, the key may not be about gender; it's about ensuring some people on the team have high social and emotional awareness or perceptiveness, not just expert knowledge or technical skills.

ACTIONS

▸ Ensure that your team has some socially intelligent women and/or team players that are effective at reading body language and social cues.

▸ Complete an individual and/or a team emotional intelligence (EQ) assessment, and set individual and team goals based on the results.

▸ Pay attention not only to what people are saying verbally, but also what they might be saying non-verbally. When you notice body language that puzzles or concerns you, get curious. Neutrally share the behaviour you observed and ask them, don't tell them, what they are thinking.
For example:

- *I notice that you have been quiet during this discussion.
  What are your thoughts on what has been said so far?*

- *I noticed you raised your eyebrows when Bill brought up his issue.
  What concerns or questions do you have about what Bill said?*

Tip #14

Reinforce critical communication abilities.

The most important trip you take in life is meeting people half way.
- Henry Boye, Author

Wageman *et al.* (2008) acknowledge that the necessary skills for the "right people" include important **communication competencies** or characteristics. Key skills include having the courage and integrity needed to bring up issues, keeping conversations confidential, and demonstrating empathy. Elaine Cox (2012), a coaching practitioner and researcher, agrees that confidentiality and empathy are keys to building trust and effective peer relationships.

Empathy is the ability to understand the content, meaning, and feeling tone of messages, and being able to reflect this back. The ability to demonstrate empathy also creates psychological safety, which is a critical component for developing trust among team members (Edmondson, 1999; 2012). Ultimately, team members need to address important issues in a confidential way that feels safe, respectful, and trustworthy for the other person. Good facilitation helps team members to actively hear others' perspectives and points of view. Without expressions of empathy, team members may not feel connected, or worse, withdraw or become defensive.

ACTIONS

▶ Ask all of your team members to reflect and consider:

- *What conversation do you need to have but are not having?*

- *Are you talking about a person rather than directly with that person?*

- *What support would you need to have a direct conversation?*

- *How could you see this issue from [that individual's, team's, or discipline's] perspective?*

▶ Individually pick one important conversation that you want to have or have been avoiding. Commit to carry it out this week using your best communication skills.

Tip #15

**Appreciate and leverage
different styles.**

You have to get along with people,
but you also have to recognize that the strength of a team is
different people with different perspectives and different personalities.
- Steve Case, Former CEO of AOL

Style assessments can be used strategically to enhance awareness of different working styles. These assessments promote conversations that help team members better understand their own personality and behavioural traits and the traits of others. Use this information to leverage individual strengths on the team and to better understand how to communicate with and influence others. Know that although there are several style assessments to choose from, the research thus far indicates that no one assessment is inherently better than any other (McKenna *et al.*, 2002:314).

ACTIONS

▶ Complete a style assessment with your team. Have a team profile produced to see team strengths and what styles are low or missing. Identify how you can mitigate any gaps in the team's profile.

▶ If you are not able to do a formal style assessment with your team, discuss:

- *Who is the person who has a strong focus on results?*

- *Who thinks through the details and considers the risks and pitfalls?*

- *Who dreams the big dreams?*

- *Who wants everyone to get along and plays a mediator role on the team?*

▶ Look at the "style" of your team by reflecting and asking if the team collectively has a tendency to be:

- *Overly analytical? Not analytical enough?*

- *Too action oriented? Not action oriented enough?*

- *Too focused on new ideas and initiatives? Not inventive enough?*

- *Too insular and internally focused? Not thinking externally enough?*

Tip #16

Be aware that even positive personality traits can be overused.

Talent wins games,
but teamwork and intelligence wins championships.
- Michael Jordan

Every **personality trait** will be more or less appropriate for a given role or situation. Any trait can turn into a negative if it is over-emphasized or mismatched with the task and/or team needs (Stock, 2004). In fact, sometimes what we call a weakness really is a strength that is being overused or used inappropriately for the situation. This is as true for the team as it is for individuals on the team. Teams, just like individuals, can suffer from blind spots and fail to realize when they are overusing certain styles, strengths, or approaches.

ACTIONS

▶ Seek a balance of different styles on the team. A style assessment that provides a team profile can help identify the diversity, or lack thereof, in your team.

▶ Help individuals pinpoint overused strengths and then help them understand the impact of this. Coach them to develop strategies to employ underused areas of strength or work with others who have strengths that complement theirs.

▶ Solicit feedback from stakeholders outside of your team to help the team members better understand their impact and how they are perceived. Ask simple, neutral questions of your stakeholders, such as:

• *What two things does this team do most effectively?*

• *What two things could this team do differently to be even more effective?*

▶ Ask your team as a whole:

• *What are we not talking about?*

• *What do we repeatedly not do because it isn't a strength for us?*

Tip #17

Ensure diversity for complex, not simple tasks.

The way a team plays as a whole determines its success.
You may have the greatest bunch of individual stars in the world,
but if they don't play together, the club won't be worth a dime.
- Babe Ruth

It is commonly believed that having a **diversity of styles** on a team is better than having a homogenous team of similar styles and personalities. That is often true, but in actual fact, it also depends on the kind of task.

For instance, Reilly *et al.* (2002) observed that when faced with complex and demanding situations, effective teams rely on team members who will challenge the norm and think differently. Team members benefit from being less attached to getting along or having others like them when discussing complex issues. However, the researchers found that when tasks are routine or require high degrees of affiliation, it is similarities and not strong differences that promote higher performance.

ACTIONS

▶ Review the key tasks and goals of your team and think about what level of style diversity is required to achieve them.

▶ For simple, routine tasks, consider putting like-minded people together to do the work.

▶ If more diversity in skills or traits is needed, invite everyone to identify what he or she could contribute more of to the team. Invite each to bring that skill or trait forward more often. Provide encouragement and reinforcement to ensure this occurs.

▶ If a high level of diversity is required for complex and innovative tasks or projects, consider soliciting or seconding outside help from other teams, consultants, or departments to enhance the diversity of your team.

Tip #18

Use your experts effectively.

Typically, **experts** need help to be effective team contributors because:

The presence of expert members may actually decrease team effectiveness if members are not helped to use the experts' special talents.
(Woolley *et al.*, 2008:16)

Do not assume that because there is an expert (someone with appreciably higher knowledge or skill) on the team that this expert person will inevitably contribute to increased team performance. In fact, the opposite is more likely true. Experts may pay less attention to others' contributions and others may give too much credence to expert views. It is equally important to have team members with a breadth of experience and strong interpersonal skills to help ensure everyone's input is considered. It is not always possible to decide who is on the team though, so make sure there are structures and processes in place so that everyone contributes and that experts do not dominate the conversations.

ACTIONS

▸ Think twice before you put the expert in charge. Their expertise is valuable. However, knowledge and technical skills do not necessarily equate to leadership skills. Assess for these skills separately.

▸ Include members with a diversity of skills and abilities that contribute to achieving the goal or task.

▸ Ensure that everyone's role and style is recognized as important for achieving your team's goals.

▸ Provide explicit instructions and confirm agreements about how members will carry out their joint work together. Don't assume this will happen naturally.

Team Behaviours

Tip #19

Make five times more positive than negative comments.

If you scatter thorns, don't go barefoot.
- Italian proverb

The highest performing teams have interactions with at least five times more (5.8 to 1) **positive than negative** comments and affirming body language signals (Frederickson and Losada, 2005). These higher performance business teams not only demonstrate greater positivity towards each other, they also have higher profitability, better customer satisfaction scores, and higher evaluations from others in the organization.

Interestingly enough, John Gottman (1994), a prolific writer and researcher on couples, also found that the same ratios predicted the success or demise of relationships. The most successful couples demonstrated a 5 to 1 positive to negative ratio, even when in conflict. In fact, 2.9 is the "Losada Line," or the ratio of positivity to negativity that separates teams and individuals who succeed from those who are less effective.

ACTIONS

▸ Bring in an independent observer to your team meeting OR observe it yourself when another team member is chairing the team meeting. Have the observer track the number of positive and negative comments and body language signals.

• When debriefing the results, ensure your team understands the financial and stakeholder satisfaction benefits of expressing positivity and ask: *"How can we foster a more positive environment to ensure results?"*

▸ Begin your remarks by making affirming comments to model positivity.

▸ Don't over-do the positive comments. Once there are more than 12 to 1 (11.6 to 1 to be exact) positive to negative comments, performance declines, possibly because there is not enough reality checking and constructive feedback occurring (Fredrickson and Losada, 2005).

Tip #20

**Foster trust behaviours
and structures.**

Some say that it takes a long time to **build trust** and about five seconds to destroy it. Trust is critical to high performing teams as evidenced by the significant body of research on trust and what it takes to develop it in successful partnerships. Trust is built through leaders and team members being consistent, reliable, respectful, open, and honest (Larson and LaFasto, 1989). Once these basics are in place, team members will be more likely to cooperate, share knowledge, and generate business results.

Frequent face-to-face and genuine communication accelerates trust, as does expressing empathy and sharing feelings, not just facts. Having a shared vision, clear roles and responsibilities, and effective team design also builds trust. Finally, clear agreements for communication, decision making, and shared norms underpin trusting and effective interpersonal relationships (Hackman and Wageman, 2005). Trust is not just about getting along well. It is also about setting up structures that facilitate trust.

ACTIONS

▸ If you are the team leader, consistently model reliable and respectful behaviour. Team members rarely exhibit more trust, reliability, or respect than their leader demonstrates. The leader sets the tone for the whole team, department, or organization.

▸ Create a feedback friendly team that regularly seeks and gives feedback to each other. Use this basic feedback model: *I see... I think... I feel... and what I would like is...*

For example:
  I see that you often work through lunch and
  I wonder what the impact is on you.
  I feel concerned that you might be overloaded with work and
  I would like to know what I can do to help.

▸ Build in more face-to-face or visual connections, not just telephone or email communication.

Tip #21

**Commit to your team
and team members.**

*Commitment with accountability closes the gap
between intention and results.*
- Sandra Gallagher, Author

High performing teams demonstrate higher interdependence and cohesion than low performers. They have a stronger **emotional commitment** to each other and a strong sense of "we-ness." These highly interdependent and cohesive teams also have a greater tolerance for conflict than lower performing teams (Tekleab, Quigley and Tesluk, 2009).

In other words, if a team is performing well, the team members also tend to have a stronger emotional bank account with each other. Having greater emotional capital with each other allows team members to work through the inevitable issues that arise in any group of people who are working together over time. Al Switzler, one of the authors of the book, *Crucial Conversations*, states this well:

In our thirty years of research and observation, one of the key findings we've uncovered is that all relationships, teams, families, and organizations have problems. The difference between the good and the best is not how many problems they have, but rather, how they resolve those problems. (Switzler, 2009)

ACTIONS

▶ Some ideas for fostering team commitment include:

- Create interdependent goals that require your team members to work together to be successful.

- Identify some logical team goals to reward, in addition to rewarding individual goals.

- Create small and frequent milestones for teams to achieve success, and acknowledge these small successes as a way to build the trust bank account (i.e., create and model a culture where both you and your team frequently catch each other doing well).

Tip #22

Take turns to leverage your collective intelligence.

Groups where a few people dominated the conversation were less collectively intelligent than those with a more equal distribution of conversational turn-taking.
(Woolley *et al.*, 2010:688)

We cannot raise individual intelligence, but we can increase the collective intelligence of a team wherein the sum is truly greater than the parts. To do this, ensure that the team uses processes that not only encourage, but also **require everyone to participate**. Try "brainsteering", a technique to ensure you identify as many individual ideas as possible. Minimize groupthink by asking open-ended questions and allowing people time to reflect on their own before contributing as a group—your reflective introverts will appreciate this (Coyne and Coyne, 2011)!

ACTIONS

▶ Follow these steps for the brainsteering technique:

- Give everyone time before a meeting and/or a few minutes during a meeting to first reflect on the issue or question to be discussed.

- Ask focused questions that invite people to look at the challenge from a different or more specific angle than you have before.

- Deliberately include everyone by giving all team members an equal chance to share their thoughts in a round robin conversation style or collaborative email exchange.

- Tell people, *"Even if you think you are being redundant, say it in your own words."* Often some unique slant or perspective is revealed from this approach.

- Ensure that everyone has about the same amount of time or space to contribute.

- Acknowledge everyone's contribution or comment with a simple, *"Thank you,"* so that nobody's comments are given more weight or value than others.

Tip #23

Communicate frequently outside of team meetings.

The more elaborate our means of communication,
the less we communicate.
- Joseph Priestley, English Chemist and Clergyman

Team meetings are critical to effectiveness but paying attention to team dynamics outside of meetings is equally if not more important. **Frequent team communication** differentiates higher performing teams from lower performing teams, according to findings from team researcher, Sandy Pentland (2012). In fact, Pentland found that the amount of team member energy and engagement outside of formal meetings has predicted up to one-third of the variation in team performance.

Encourage team members to connect outside of meetings as much as they do within their meetings. Support peers to work with and learn from each other as much or even more than they seek guidance from their leader.

ACTIONS

▶ Foster frequent and informal team communication by booking some in-person "coffee breaks" together for the team to interact informally on a weekly or bi-weekly basis.

▶ If you are a virtual team, book some virtual "coffee breaks" together for the team to interact informally on a weekly or bi-weekly basis.

▶ Verbally acknowledge and appreciate members who are connecting outside of meetings productively.

▶ Signal the importance of connecting outside of team meetings by doing so yourself and commenting on the value of this at your next team meeting.

Tip #24

Actively solicit ideas from new and returning team members.

Ideas come from everything.
- Alfred Hitchcock, Filmmaker

Teams can sometimes struggle to solicit and use **new and re-turning team members' ideas** effectively (LaFasto and Larson, 2001). This means it is all too easy for teams to lose and/or not integrate fresh ideas and insights that becomes available to them (Gruenfeld, 2000).

In essence, if they are not deliberate and mindful, teams "carry on carrying on." They stick to their typical routines and stay in their usual patterns of interpersonal interaction. Thus, it is critical for teams to make a conscious effort to welcome the insights and ideas of new or returning team members.

ACTIONS

▸ Ensure that you ask new team members for their perspective, or what they found worked well in their previous job that might benefit this team or situation.

▸ Ask your returning team member about the team culture:

- *What do you notice is the same or new about how the team is interacting together?*

- *What do you see the team doing that seems to support team effectiveness?*

- *What do you notice the team doing that seems to impede team performance?*

▸ Explicitly invite your returning member to give a presentation on what he or she learned and make one to three key recommendations about what the individual would suggest the team adopt, improve, or do more or less of as a team. Start the team conversation by publically appreciating the risk the returning member is taking to share his or her observations and suggestions.

Tip #25

Collaborate to save time and costs.

If the collaboration efficiency of only 20 of the less efficient project managers and organizational leaders improved from below-average to average, it would save the roughly 400 individuals who interacted regularly with those managers and leaders up to 1,500 hours per week.
- Results of a six-year organizational study (Cross *et al.*, 2010)

Formal accountability structures are important but they are not enough in today's innovative and intersecting teams and companies. It is these informal **collaboration** networks and spontaneous interactions between people who see problems from different perspectives that are helpful. What's more, people often draw on their networks to successfully execute plans, particularly when the path to success is not obvious or becomes more complicated than expected.

ACTIONS

▶ Create opportunities between teams to foster networking, collaboration and innovation.

▶ Identify explicit working agreements that foster collaboration both within the team and with other teams.

▶ Ask team members to seek input from inside and outside the team and set up a time and structure to share that information in the team.

▶ Ask each team member to connect with someone outside of his or her usual circle. This networking approach will invite and encourage more innovative ideas to surface.

▶ Experiment together on ways to collaborate, and allow for testing and revisiting of ideas and approaches.

Tip #26

Solicit different views; don't be redundant.

*Dialogue is a process of genuine interaction through which
human beings listen to each other deeply enough
to be changed by what they learn.*
- Hal Saunders, Former U.S. Diplomat

Years of research and dozens of studies continue to highlight that ineffective groups and teams tend to spend most of their time discussing redundant information that is already shared by the group members. Effective groups spend far more time discussing information known only to one or a minority of members. It is often this unique information that is most important to the team's success (Mesmer-Magnus and DeChurch, 2009).

Openness and participation help team members reveal conflicting and unique perspectives (Mesmer-Magnus and DeChurch, 2009). Since this does not usually happen naturally in teams, the leader or team coach needs to set up systems that **encourage different opinions**. The key to success is to provide structure to conversations and meetings.

ACTIONS

▶ In your meetings, ask open-ended questions that solicit different views, opinions, and ideas, such as:

- *What is not being said?*

- *What is a different view or perspective?*

- *What could we have missed here?*

- *Who outside of our team might have some information that we might be missing? How can we get access to this information or perspective?*

- *What were the benefits of this meeting?*

- *What are some concerns coming out of this meeting?*

- *When you leave this meeting, what will be your thoughts about it?*

- *What do we need to do differently next time to get more views on the table?*

Tip #27

Frame decisions in objective terms.

A meta-analysis of 72 independent studies identified that teams tend to perform better when they are engaged in "intellective tasks" (Mesmer-Magnus and DeChurch, 2009). Intellective tasks and **decisions** have relatively **correct or objective answers** that are based on facts and rational reasoning (e.g., math problems) versus tasks that are based on subjective judgment or opinion (e.g., what team training to pursue for the year).

One way to frame a problem to be more "intellective" is to create common, agreed upon criteria to objectively evaluate what otherwise could be a subjective decision. Team members can take turns presenting and asking questions about the issue before discussing potential solutions or options. This approach supports the team to come to a more objective answer based on common information and explicit criteria versus a judgmental answer based on team members' status, opinions or preferences.

ACTIONS

▶ Use a structure such as the Grid Analysis below and work as a team to list potential solutions and criteria for evaluating the solutions BEFORE engaging in the decision making discussion. Then, individually assign a number (1 to 3, low to high) based on how well each solution meets each criterion. Compare and discuss your ratings. Add the ratings to identify the highest scoring solution, then confirm agreement on this solution.

For Example:

Issue: What team training should we pursue this year?

Criteria / Option	Urgent issues in this area	New training for people	Team interest in topic	Fees within training budget	Total Score
Performance Management	1	2	2	3	8
Conflict Resolution	3	1	1	2	7
Change Management	3	3	1	2	9

Tip #28

Shift your thinking from indifferent to empathetic.

Before we can truly understand another person,
we must walk a mile in their moccasins.
Before we can walk in their moccasins,
we must take off our own.
- Native American Proverb

Pate and Shoblom (2013) have identified a technique that allows individuals to effectively shift their thinking from **indifferent to empathetic**, especially when there is high conflict among team members that causes people to disengage. Indifference, or apathy, is counter-productive to effective team performance. In contrast, empathy is a key behaviour of effective team members (Wageman *et al.*, 2008). To avoid apathy, challenge assumptions, clarify values and priorities, and expand the set of viable action steps. This can decrease indifference and increase the likelihood of empathetic behaviour in teams.

ACTIONS

▸ Try these three techniques to shift the team's conversational style, starting with your own style.

- Challenge your own assumptions about what you are thinking or doing. Ask:

  o *How do I know this is true?*

- Be aware of values, concerns and priorities for different individuals. Consider:

  o *What do I know is important to this person? Given this, how does his or her position make sense?*

- Identify possible courses of action. Ask:

  o *What other possibilities exist here and are inclusive of what we collectively want?*

Tip #29

Actively encourage "teaming" behaviours.

Do what you can to show you care about other people
and you will make our world a better place.
- Rosalynn Carter, Former American First Lady

Team researcher Amy Edmondson (2012) uses **"teaming"** as a verb to represent a general team mindset and the collaborative, "in the moment" behaviours that support team performance in ever-changing circumstances. Teams need to plan, team build, learn, and execute all at the same time. It is a bit like building a house while already living in it.

Three important teaming skills required to be effective in 21st century teams include: interpersonal awareness, making inquiries at the right moments, and being able to teach others what you know.

ACTIONS

▶ Model and implement these three key teaming behaviours:

- Use your intuition to make a tentative guess about the deeper meanings behind what people are saying. Note people's tone, body language, and emotions as well as the words spoken.

- Ask open-ended questions clearly and frequently.

- Increase the time you spend teaching and mentoring others.

▶ Get feedback from others on one action that would help you improve your teaming skills.

▶ Be willing to share knowledge faster, more frequently and in accessible ways to people outside your area of expertise.

▶ Take an Emotional Intelligence (EQ) assessment and identify areas that you could develop. These skills are needed more than ever in fast-moving and ever-changing teams.

Tip #30

Leverage task conflict to improve innovation and effectiveness.

I didn't say it was your fault.
I said I was going to blame you.
- Anonymous

Task conflict occurs when people do not agree on the work that is being done. In contrast, interpersonal conflict is a more personally oriented type of conflict that occurs when people take issue with someone's personality style, the approach he or she takes to working, or his or her way of interacting. Interpersonal conflict can be difficult to sort out and can feel like blame. However, moderate levels of task conflict can actually enhance team performance because it may encourage multiple perspectives and new ideas.

Many studies have found that decision making effectiveness improves when team members share unique information (Hackman, 2011; Mesmer-Magnus and DeChurch, 2009). Further, constructive debate can lead to innovation. From this perspective, it is important to help team members find a way to express alternate views productively and not take differences personally. An acronym for remembering this is QTIP (Quit Taking It Personally).

ACTIONS

▶ Questions to ask your team to address task conflict could include:

- *How could we use or bring together all of our ideas in an innovative way?*
- *What is one thing you like about this approach, task, or idea?*
- *What is one thing you think would improve this approach, task, or idea?*
- *If we had to implement each one of these ideas or solutions, how could we make each one work?*
- *What are the areas of disagreement that interfere with us getting this done?*
- *What else is preventing us from getting this task done effectively?*
- *Where do we have overlaps on this task that continually get in our way?*

▶ Focus on the issue, not the person, when discussing concerns.

Tip #31

Ask, don't just advocate.

When things get too complicated,
it sometimes makes sense to stop and wonder:
Have I asked the right question?
- Enrico Bombieri, Author and Mathematician

Asking questions is as important for high performing teams as it is for individuals. The researchers Frederickson and Losada (2005) observed that team members in high performing teams make inquiries (i.e., ask questions) as often as they advocate or make the case for their own position, demonstrating a one-to-one inquiry to advocacy ratio.

Questions are important for enhancing learning, stimulating innovation, and deepening conversations. Good questioners have a mindset of being curious and coming from a position of not knowing. Key questioning skills include stating hypotheses or guesses tentatively rather than definitively, checking for understanding, and asking for clarification. Remember, he (or she) who asks the questions holds the power!

ACTIONS

▸ Role model and teach your team how to ask open-ended questions. This will support your team members to be actively curious about each other's perspective.

▸ Remember that open-ended questions typically begin with "how" or "what." "Closed" questions that have a clear "yes" or "no" or one word answer are less effective.

▸ Reduce your use of "why," since it can often provoke defensiveness. Ask "what" or "how" questions instead, such as:

- *What influenced you to...?*

- *What factors did you consider?*

- *How did you come to your decision?*

Tip #32

Focus on strengths to build engagement.

Wise leaders invest in **strengths**. If a workplace is only focused on what is not working and how to improve, the likelihood of employees being engaged is a mere nine per cent. Instead, if the leadership highlights and builds on the strengths of its staff, approximately 73 per cent will be engaged (Gallop Q12 study in Buckingham and Coffman, 1999).

A strength-based team approach includes finding out what people love to do and then helping them do more of it. When teams work like this, it seems easier and more engaging for everyone. A strength-based team approach also includes being compassionate with one another regarding the minor areas each person needs to manage, and selecting complementing team members who are strong in areas where others are weak.

ACTIONS

▶ Have a conversation with each individual on your team and ask:

- *What percentage of the time do you find yourself using your natural strengths at work?*

- *How frequently are you doing what you love to do at work?*

- *How well do you think you leverage other team members' natural strengths?*

- *How could you do more of what you love and still meet your business goals?*

▶ Have a conversation as a team and take turns sharing individual strengths. Discuss ways to capitalize on these strengths.

▶ Lead an activity where team members identify one strength they appreciate about each other. This activity can be done either verbally or in writing. If writing strengths, give each person a card and have them write his or her name on it. Pass the card to the right and allow two minutes for people to write a strength for the person whose card they have. Continue until the card returns to the person. Have someone external to the team facilitate if you are uncomfortable leading this activity within the team.

Tip #33

Be open-minded.

The mind that opens to a new idea
never returns to its original size.
- Albert Einstein

LaFasto and Larson (2001) explored what makes teams work best and found that team members particularly value the quality of openness in other team members. Openness includes being receptive to new ideas and feedback from others. It is important to ensure that team members are open to each other's ideas and acknowledge the value of each other's perspectives. The key is to seek to understand before being understood.

Team members are most effective when they practice coming from the perspective of a learner's mind of "not knowing" and seek to learn something new in every conversation. To be even more effective, it can be helpful to let the other person know what was learned as a result of the conversation with them.

ACTIONS

▶ Try making comments and asking questions that signal openness, such as:

- *What I appreciate about your idea is…*

- *What your perspective made me think about or wonder is…*

- *Please tell me what you like most about what I have said.*

- *What is one thing that would improve my idea?*

- *What is one thing that would make me even more effective in working with you?*

- *What really caught my attention when you spoke was…*

- *I wasn't thinking about the issue that way – tell me more.*

- *Interesting. Tell me more.*

▶ Demonstrate curiosity by asking questions at least as much as you answer them.

Tip #34

Acknowledge or agree before critiquing.

A pessimist sees the difficulty in every opportunity;
an optimist sees the opportunity in every difficulty.
- Winston Churchill

Agreeableness is a valuable trait for team members to have and it is the extent to which team members are good-natured, gentle, co-operative, forgiving, and hopeful. These traits are in direct contrast to team members who demonstrate irritable, ruthless, suspicious, unco-operative, or inflexible behaviours (Reilly, Lynn and Aronson, 2002).

While different opinions need to be heard, having team members who habitually take on a naysayer role or who are constantly critical is not helpful. This refers back to the Losada line in Tip #19. Individuals who demonstrate positive to negative comments and body language at a level below the Losada line of 2.9 to 1 are less successful than those who achieve a ratio above this line (Losada and Heaphy, 2004).

ACTIONS

▶ A simple way to demonstrate more agreeableness is to state at least two things you agree with or like first, wait for a response and then decide if you still want to offer what you don't agree with or like.

▶ If you can't find anything to authentically agree with in a person's idea or comment, at least find something positive to acknowledge about his or her idea or perspective, or appreciate his or her good intentions. Try:

  • *It looks like you have given this idea a lot of thought.*

  • *I appreciate how you are looking for ways to improve this situation.*

  • *I can see that you are passionate about this idea.*

▶ Replace "no" or "but" with **"yes, and…"**

Tip #35

Be conscientious, responsible, and organized.

It's not that I'm so smart,
it's just that I stay with problems longer.
- Albert Einstein

Conscientiousness is another valued trait of team members (Barrick, 2001; McKenna, 2002) and can be defined as the extent to which team members are careful, thorough, achievement-oriented, responsible, organized, self-disciplined, and steadfast to commitments.

On the other hand, sometimes individuals who are naturally creative and spontaneous have difficulty being conscientious. These more carefree individuals should take care to preserve these positive traits. At the same time, if they are the less organized team members, they need to realize that good intentions to be organized will not be enough. Remember that people judge themselves by their intentions, but they judge others by their behaviours. In other words, it is important for team members to move beyond good intentions and to demonstrate a level of conscientiousness that is acceptable to others.

ACTIONS

▶ If you are not naturally an organized person, dedicate some time for organizational planning each day and develop personal systems such as integrated calendars, reminders, and use of task lists.

▶ As a team leader, coach your less organized team members to maintain a basic level of organization and responsibility. Include this as a performance measure.

▶ Once again, clear working agreements amongst team members can support your team to know where it is most important to be organized, and where they can be more flexible and fluid.

Tip #36

Scan for new ideas outside the team.

Ideas can come from anyone, and anywhere,
if you as a leader design an "architecture of participation"
that allows talented individuals to create together.
- Bill Taylor, Co-founder of *Fast Company* magazine

The most successful teams focus their **learning externally**, not just internally. These high performing teams have been dubbed "X teams" by Ancona and Bresman (2007). "X teams" are encouraged to network outside of their team and bring back important ideas, which help the team to avoid unnecessary mistakes, increase its competency, and improve its level of innovation. Research highlights that high performing teams reach out beyond their membership to gather information, coordinate tasks, establish cooperative relationships, and advocate for their team's goals.

ACTIONS

▶ Set up the expectation and structure for your team to actively look for and solicit outside information.

▶ Encourage and provide support for team members to spend a dedicated amount of time each month networking outside of the team and the organization.

▶ Schedule five to ten minutes in team meetings for a "Trends Watch." Ask:

- *What have you heard or read lately that might impact or inform our team's work?*

- *What trends are happening around us that spark new ideas for our team's work?*

- *What is one interesting idea that you heard or read lately that really made you think differently?*

▶ Invite individuals from other teams to present about their work, profession, or department to your team.

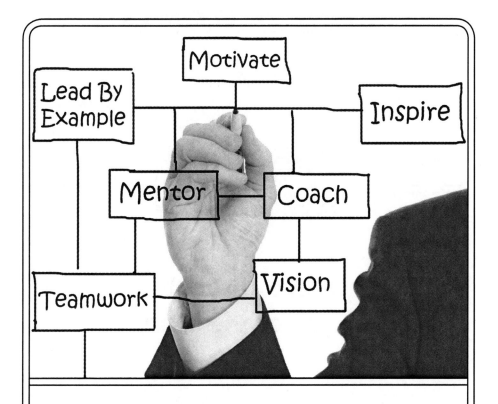

Team Coaching

Tip #37

Leverage the natural cycles of the team.

Coming together is a beginning.
Keeping together is progress.
Working together is success.
- Henry Ford

Pay attention to the natural **cycles** of a team, which occur at the beginning, midpoint, and ending of a team's natural or defined project, work or task. Team beginnings offer an opportunity for the team to start out with a clear, correct and shared understanding. Midpoints are when teams may want to "come up for air" and refocus to ensure they are on track for success. Endings are an important time to reflect and learn.

These three key points in a team cycle are the most effective times to intervene or coach a team. Intervening at times other than these points of a team's natural work cycle tends to be less effective and may even be disruptive (Gersick, 1988). Thus intervening at times other than beginnings, midpoints and endings may waste both the coach's and the team's time.

ACTIONS

▸ Set clear beginnings for your team with goals and strategies, along with defined milestones and final deadlines, to create natural midpoint and ending cycles that will support your team to better plan and track its work. Creating defined cycles is especially important for leadership teams and non-project teams who do not have natural milestones and deadlines.

▸ Leverage the departures or additions of team members to create new beginnings for a team and start a new team cycle.

▸ Review and revise plans, strategies, working agreements, and goals if required at the natural midpoint of your team's work together.

▸ Once a major task or project is done, celebrate with your team but don't stop there. Debrief what you learned about team strengths and what could have been done differently to be even more effective and successful.

Tip #38

**Accelerate performance
at team beginnings.**

The beginning is the most important part of the work.
- Plato, *The Republic*

There is a saying that goes, "Don't wait for a fire before buying a fire extinguisher." The same can be said for **team coaching**, which is becoming a more common service and intervention in organizations over the last 10 to 15 years.

If a team is considering bringing in an external coach to support its development, it is important to know that external coaches can have a higher impact when they are brought in at the beginning of a team's cycle. This is true for a team that is newly forming, re-forming with new team members, or even resetting to deliver a new strategy, project, or change. Starting coaching at team beginnings is most powerful because it helps leaders create the right conditions for effectiveness and supports a team to launch properly (Hackman, 2011).

ACTIONS

▶ Invest wisely by assigning a coach to your team early on in its formation. It's like fertilizing and tilling the soil before planting seeds.

▶ If you bring in an external coach at a time other than a naturally occurring new starting point for the team, create a new beginning by developing a new focus, new set of goals, or new strategy upon which the team can refocus.

▶ If you choose to pursue external coaching, ensure you select a coach who specializes in working with teams and has a background in and strong knowledge of team effectiveness principles.

Tip #39

Use team coaching to identify the team brand and strengths.

*I think what coaching is all about
is taking players and analyzing their ability,
and putting them in a position where they can excel
within the framework of the team winning.*
- Don Shula, American Football Coach

Team coaching can help teams be even higher performing, and can assist them to leverage their strengths to better achieve their goals. "We found very few teams that were able to decode their successes and failures and learn from them without intervention from a leader or another team coach" (Wageman *et al.*, 2008:161). Reviewing successes and the behaviours that contributed to the successes is a great way to identify team strengths. Promote these strengths within the team and with others to influence the team brand or reputation in the organization.

ACTIONS

▶ Ask a coach or individuals outside of the team who have often worked with your team for their observations about strengths your team demonstrates.

▶ If you don't have assistance, identify one or two signature strengths as a team. Consider what your team does exceptionally well by asking:

- *What do others say they like about our team?*

- *What recognition has our team received from others?*

- *What reputation does our team seem to have in the organization?*

- *What values seem to come through more than others in our team's work and how do these values show up as strengths? (e.g., results oriented, detail focused, easy to work with, etc.)*

- *When does our team work easily together and discussions flow readily? Does this flow state give clues about a natural strength for our team?*

Tip #40

Address the three most dysfunctional team behaviours swiftly.

Felps, Mitchell, and Byington (2006) researched what factors cause team conflict and have determined that there are three primary styles of **dysfunctional behaviours** that are most toxic:

1. Withholding effort.
2. Over-expressing negative emotions and attitudes.
3. Violating agreed upon norms.

The whole team may become negative, distrusting, and defensive, even if only one person is demonstrating any of these three dysfunctional behaviours.

Act swiftly if any team members demonstrate one or more of these three dysfunctional behaviours as this will potentially impact the team's performance. Unfortunately, even one dysfunctional individual can be the bad apple that spoils the whole barrel, or team in this case.

ACTIONS

▶ Consider the group dynamics of your team and the contributions of individual team members to those dynamics. Ask yourself:

- *Are there team members who sabotage your team's best efforts?*

- *Do any team members pull the group down?*

- *Do any team members blatantly disregard working agreements?*

▶ If any of these issues are occurring, consider coaching to help you assertively get on top of these issues before they get on top of you. Don't wait to address issues or the time you'll need to do so will double or triple.

▶ It may be necessary to put a performance improvement plan in place for negative or dysfunctional team members. Don't make rules for the whole team to address only one person's poor performance, attitude, or behaviour.

Tip #41

Coach each other,
don't just gossip and vent.

*I've always believed that a lot of the troubles in the
world would disappear if we were talking to
each other instead of about each other.*
- Ronald Reagan, 40th President of the United States

Hackman and O'Connor's (2005) research suggests that **peer coaching** has one of the strongest correlations to team effectiveness compared to any other team intervention they studied. Similarly, Elaine Cox, a coaching practitioner and researcher, says that, "Peer coaching taps into a source of less costly, in-house expertise, and support that is highly relevant and readily available in the workplace" (Cox, 2012:428).

The impact of peer relationships on employee engagement has also been steadily rising over the last few years (The Corporate Executive Board Company, 2012). Research indicates that employees particularly appreciate it when their colleagues help them translate corporate goals into their everyday work and give them informal feedback, both of which are key aspects of peer coaching.

Peer coaching can include having peers support each other to remain accountable to their working agreements when they see any agreements being transgressed. It makes sense to have peers support peers because team leaders simply do not have time to do it all themselves.

ACTIONS

▶ Set the conditions for peer coaching to be successful by providing your team with training in coaching skills and giving team members explicit permission to coach each other.

▶ Formalize peer coaching by having individuals set aside time to coach each other and/or make it informal, encouraging your team members to go to each other for support when they need it.

Tip #42

Implement a "half-time team huddle."

If we could first know where we are, and whither we are tending,
we could better judge what to do and how to do it.
- Abraham Lincoln

Team learning and reflection does not often happen on its own, and it entails more than just talking about what went wrong or what went right. The **half-time team huddle** is a popular team coaching technique to pause a conversation, interaction, or even a meeting (Hawkins, 2010). This technique often effectively shifts a dynamic that needs changing and supports people to observe "how" the group is working together, not just "what" they are talking about.

Actively use the huddles to allow the team to reset and change course if needed or do more of what is working well. Ensure that the huddles happen even more often when interactions are going well so that the team can acknowledge and build strengths, not just reflect on problem interactions or inefficiencies.

ACTIONS

▶ Instructions to initiate a half-time huddle are as follows:

1. Pause your meeting to ask:

   • *What is one thing that is going well so far?*

   • *What is one thing you would change?*

2. Don't discuss and debate what people say. If it is a conversation or meeting with more than two people, do a round robin and ensure everyone speaks.

3. Respond to team members' answers with a simple *"Thank you."*

4. When everyone is done, recap the themes, set any actions to address the things to change, and then continue on.

Tip #43

Align individual coaching with team goals.

I've worked too hard and too long
to let anything stand in the way of my goals.
I will not let my teammates down and I will not let myself down.
- Mia Hamm, American Soccer Player

Team coaching, while focused on the team, can include some specific, **individual coaching** of the leader and/or other members when individual support could help them perform effectively on the team. Many coaching models also include individual coaching of the team members as part of the team coaching (Anderson *et al.*, 2008; Blattner and Bacigalupo, 2007; Clutterbuck, 2007; Haug, 2011; Mulec and Roth, 2005).

In particular, individual coaching is a key way to support the team leader to be most effective in leading and guiding the team. Sometimes peer coaching is the most helpful strategy. But other times, meeting one-on-one with each member of the team to support them to achieve success in alignment with the team's mutual goals can prove more effective.

ACTIONS

▶ Will individual coaching for one or more of your team members be beneficial for your team? Ask:

- *Will team coaching alone get you where you need to go?*

- *How can you best align individual goals with team level goals?*

- *Are there skills, behaviours or mindsets that individuals on your team need to develop in a concentrated manner outside of your team coaching?*

- *Who is a high performer who might have the potential to be even more influential with a little bit of extra support?*

- *Who is performing slightly below his or her potential right now but appears to have the capability to improve with some extra support and coaching?*

Virtual Teams

Tip #44

Overcome the lack of non-verbal communication cues.

Verbal and non-verbal cues play a key role in team social interaction and these are often missing in virtual teams. This lack of cues can make it hard to get to know other team members and to be effective. For instance, Johnson and his colleagues studied virtual teams and quoted a team member who felt disconnected from her virtual team members:

> We never got too personal—others in the team did not know I was pregnant until the last week of class. This is something that would have been obvious if we were meeting face-to-face, but it just never came up online. (Johnson *et al.*, 2002:386)

Further, people are more likely to misinterpret communication in a virtual setting because there is less access to important visual and body language cues. In addition, research shows that individuals do not share their feelings as readily in virtual environments. Rather, there is a better tacit or intuitive feel for what is happening when people meet face-to-face because individuals "signal" empathy, trust, and connection through voice tone and body language, which helps them get in sync with others.

ACTIONS

▸ Take the time to get to know and socialize with your virtual team members similar to the way you would in the office. Consider scheduling virtual coffee breaks and lunch dates so that your virtual team members can connect informally.

▸ Pay attention when there are signs of discord simmering. Conflict takes longer to build up on a virtual team and leaders often don't notice or attend to the early signs. Once the conflict has reached a "full boil" it takes longer to bring it down.

▸ Pick up the phone for tricky conversations - emotional tone is lost in email and it's too easy for conflict to escalate and go viral over email and in social forums.

▸ Build in face-to-face gatherings at least once or twice a year.

Tip #45

Structure virtual teams for greater interaction.

The single biggest problem in communication
is the illusion that it has taken place.
- George Bernard Shaw

Potter and Balthazard (2002) found that in virtual teams, the **style of interaction** is as important at predicting success as it is in face-to-face teams. In other words, whether the team is in-person or virtual, how the members interact will determine the quality of the solutions generated and how well ideas are accepted by the team.

Virtual teams benefit from structured processes and techniques in and between meetings as much as or even more so than in person teams. Ensure that every team member has a chance to speak in virtual meetings and that there are many round-robin check-ins to hear all team members' perspectives on key discussions and decisions.

ACTIONS

▶ Consider having different team members own different parts of meeting agendas so that there is greater ownership for virtual meetings.

▶ Working agreements become especially critical for virtual teams. Ask team members to prepare to discuss questions such as:

- *What kinds of interaction and communication will keep you connected to the team?*

- *What behaviours and agreements will support you to be as effective as possible with the other team members?*

- *What is one pet peeve you have? Something that makes you feel less productive when others engage in this behaviour?*

Tip #46

Become social media savvy to stay in contact.

An article in *Harvard Business Review* described how the use of **social media** can help dissimilar people work more effectively together (Ferrazi, 2012). Ferrazi specifically described the Xilinx high tech company, an organization that has used social media effectively to enhance team performance. Xilinx reported a 25 per cent increase in engineer productivity thanks to social media tools that encouraged and enabled collaborative employee activities.

Using social media well also helps create greater predictability of communication among team members, which is important for building safety and trust. In Ferrazi's (2012) study of globally distributed teams, the teams with unpredictable communication patterns and fewer team members participating in the discussions experienced less trust than teams with predictable communication patterns.

ACTIONS

▸ Agree upon social media platforms, instant messaging and webinar tools to use as a team and put processes and usage expectations in place.

▸ Exchange personal as well as professional information through a common platform to help create bonding and identification with the other team members.

▸ Do a quick "Take Five" at the beginning of a meeting to give people an opportunity to share information about what is happening in their lives.

▸ Focus on consistent, predictable communication and reporting that highlights quality, not quantity, so people don't get overloaded with emails and administrivia.

▸ Agree upon timelines for responses to calls and emails, and the format and frequency for updates so people know what to expect from each other.

Success Measures

Tip #47

Solicit stakeholder feedback to set goals and measure success.

Team coach Peter Hawkins (2011) proposes that team coaching is most powerful when there is a balance between an internal focus on the team's functioning and an external focus on **stakeholder relationships and performance expectations**. Hawkins' approach can be characterized as having an "outside-in" and "future-back" focus for the team. Teams need to ensure that external stakeholder expectations are addressed and that they influence the goals and the way the team works together. Stakeholder expectations are front and center in high performing teams, influencing both the team's goals and the actions required to take them there.

This internal-external balance is confirmed by Wageman *et al.* (2008) who found that the highest performing senior leadership teams are guided by leaders who have as much of an external focus as an internal one.

ACTIONS

▸ Ask team stakeholders, via conversations or surveys, questions such as:

- *What do you most need from this team currently?*

- *What do you need in the future from this team?*

- *How do you measure success for this team?*

- *How well is this team meeting your expectations on a scale of 1 to 10? ("Almost never" to "Almost always meets expectations")*

- *If this team was meeting all your expectations, what would it be doing?*

▸ Complete a stakeholder map with the team, identifying the key individuals, teams, clients, customers, suppliers, etc. with whom the team interacts. Identify strategies for best interacting and communicating with these stakeholders, as indicated in the example below.

Stakeholder Name	Stakeholder Needs of Team	Team Needs of Stakeholder	Style / Approach	Objections / Concerns	Actions / Communication Approach

Tip #48

Measure HOW the team is working, not just WHAT is achieved.

If we do what is necessary, all the odds are in our favour.
- Henry Kissinger, Nobel Peace Prize Recipient

Just having the right team inputs does not automatically ensure that the team will achieve the right outputs or results, as it is not a directly linear relationship (Losada, 2008). In other words, **HOW *a team works together*** will influence the team's success just as much as *WHAT* it actually does.

How a team works together includes who speaks, when they speak, who influences whom, and who decides what. It includes the roles individuals take, agreements they consciously make, and even unconscious patterns and habits that shape how the team works together. Paying attention to the team's interaction patterns and dynamics, after the team design, structure, and conditions are well set up, will contribute to team success.

ACTIONS

▶ Identify measures of success to track how effectively the team is working together. Although team interaction can be difficult to quantify and measure, some potential measures include:

• Overall meeting effectiveness ratings of 80 per cent or higher, as rated by team members at the end of each meeting.

• Participation of each team member at least once in every team meeting.

• Decrease in the number of times people are interrupted in the meetings.

• Frequency that team members solicit input and information from people outside of the team on major decisions.

• Decrease in the average amount of time taken to make a team decision.

• Decrease in the number of team decisions that are revisited and rehashed.

• Decrease in the number of miscommunications per week.

• Increase in the speed to resolve issues constructively.

Tip #49

Review team learning regularly to be agile.

*Even a mistake may turn out to be the one thing
necessary to a worthwhile achievement.*

- Henry Ford

Many team coaching and team effectiveness practitioners indicate that teams cannot leave learning together to chance (Clutterbuck, 2007; Hawkins, 2011; Hackman, 2003). Teams need to consciously decide on a process to **encourage learning** because they often get caught up in doing and forget to take time for reflecting.

Continuous improvement is driven by the deliberate review of what has worked and what has not. This kind of team learning differentiates the teams that continually evolve and grow from teams that stagnate because they do not examine and reflect on their ways of working and assumptions.

ACTIONS

▶ Some strategies for structuring team learning include:

- Set out learning goals in a team learning and development plan.

- Critically review what has been learned together at regular, scheduled intervals. Try asking every team member to write down one thing that worked well and one thing that did not work well or could be improved. Then go around and listen to each person's answer or alternatively, if safety and trust is low, collect the written answers and read them aloud (without names attached).

- Take time at the end of every team meeting to do a round robin for 30 seconds per person to identify one thing that team members learned during the meeting.

Tip #50

Assess team effectiveness regularly.

The time to repair the roof is when the sun is shining.
- John F. Kennedy

We found in our research that **team assessment** is an important and highly-valued component of team coaching, both at the beginning of coaching to benchmark the team's current state, and at the end of the coaching to identify and measure progress (Carr and Peters, 2012). Other team coaching researchers and team effectiveness experts agree (Clutterbuck, 2007; Wageman *et al.*, 2005).

When choosing a team assessment tool, consider whether it is based on reliable team effectiveness and coaching research. If not, then ensure it provides a meaningful and easy-to-understand approach for using the information functionally and practically. An assessment tool to consider is the *High Performance Team Effectiveness Assessment* (Peters, 2013).

ACTIONS

▶ Take the time to assess how effectively your team is working together with a formal assessment or informally by asking questions like:

- *Overall, how effectively does our team work together?*
  Use a scale of 1 to 10, from not effective at all to totally effective.

- *What two things does our team do that contribute most to its success?*

- *How active are all team members at participating in meetings?*

- *How prepared are team members for meetings?*

- *What is one specific example of something you learned from our team that you probably would not have learned on your own? Vice versa?*

- *What are two things our team could do differently to be even more effective?*

Conclusion

Conclusion

Ultimately,
every team is unique.

I cannot do everything, but I will not let what
I cannot do interfere with what I can do.
- Edward Everett Hale, American Author

There is a lot of research about what makes teams effective and we have presented some key points in *50 Tips for Terrific Teams*. Of course, knowing the tips isn't enough; now it's time to make sure that you USE them, too!

Despite some commonalities in findings and some suggestions about good practices, what works on one team doesn't necessarily work on another. **Ultimately, every team is unique**. What makes teams interesting is that they develop and change over time, thus requiring different approaches at different times (McGrath *et al.*, 2000). Teams do not move towards their goals in straightforward, linear ways. Wageman *et al.*'s (2008) recommendation to set up conditions that are likely to enhance team effectiveness is important, but success is not guaranteed. Team effectiveness is always a journey and requires vigilant care and attention to the structures of success, the people on the team, and the processes that support the team to be productive.

Teams are inherently complex and every team has to work within its own unique culture and context. This makes achieving team effectiveness a result of many interweaving factors, not just one factor in isolation (Hackman, 2012; Rico *et al.*, 2011). As a team leader, you can effectively coach your own team if you put the time and attention on how the team is working, not just what it is doing. However, it also may be helpful to have a coach from outside the team work with you to review your team effectiveness, as it can be hard to see the water when you are the fish immersed in it!

A powerful resource is our research-based *High Performance Team Coaching* system. It integrates some of these 50 tips and provides a clear framework for team coaching that effectively influences team performance. The system is not just for coaches though; it supports team leaders to coach their own teams and HR professionals to become trusted, knowledgeable partners who can coach their clients more effectively.

No matter what your team and leadership goals are, a trained team coach can assist you to benchmark where your team is today, set goals for where you want to be, and put the structures, behaviours and mindset in place for you and your team to achieve your ideal future.

For more information on our *High Performance Team Coaching* system, any of the 50 tips, or our leadership and team coaching services, visit our websites:

www.InnerActiveLeadership.ca
www.CatherineCarr.ca
www.HighPerformanceTeamCoaching.com

Thanks for reading and please let us know how these tips help your team to reach even higher levels of performance and effectiveness!

Jacqueline and Catherine

50 Tips for Terrific Teams

© Peters and Carr, 2013

Team Design and Structure
- #1: Learn what makes a team effective.
- #2: Determine if you are a group or a team.
- #3: Set the conditions for team success.
- #4: Maximize effectiveness by having 10 members or less.
- #5: Create a strong team design and structure.
- #6: Get real about the information, time, and resources your goals require.
- #7: Hold an effective team launch.
- #8: Create a Team Charter.
- #9: Set norms and working agreements.
- #10: Refresh the team with a relaunch.
- #11: Address team dysfunction quickly.

Team Players
- #12: Choose or develop the right players.
- #13: Select women… and men with emotional and social intelligence.
- #14: Reinforce critical communication abilities.
- #15: Appreciate and leverage different styles.
- #16: Be aware that even positive personality traits can be overused.
- #17: Ensure diversity for complex, not simple tasks.
- #18: Use your experts effectively.

Team Behaviours
- #19: Make five times more positive than negative comments.
- #20: Foster trust behaviours and structures.
- #21: Commit to your team and team members!
- #22: Take turns to leverage your collective intelligence.
- #23: Communicate frequently outside of team meetings.
- #24: Actively solicit ideas from new and returning team members.
- #25: Collaborate to save time and costs.
- #26: Solicit different views; don't be redundant.
- #27: Frame decisions in objective terms.
- #28: Shift your thinking from indifferent to empathetic.
- #29: Actively encourage "teaming" behaviours.
- #30: Leverage task conflict to improve innovation and effectiveness.
- #31: Ask, don't just advocate.
- #32: Focus on strengths to build engagement.
- #33: Be open-minded.
- #34: Acknowledge or agree before critiquing.
- #35: Be conscientious, responsible, and organized.
- #36: Scan for new ideas outside the team.

www.HighPerformanceTeamCoaching.com

Team Coaching

#37: Leverage the natural cycles of the team.
#38: Accelerate performance at team beginnings.
#39: Use team coaching to identify the team brand and strengths.
#40: Address the three most dysfunctional team behaviours swiftly.
#41: Coach each other, don't just gossip and vent.
#42: Implement a "half-time team huddle."
#43: Align individual coaching with team goals.

Virtual Teams

#44: Overcome the lack of non-verbal communication cues.
#45: Structure virtual teams for greater interaction.
#46: Become social media savvy to stay in contact.

Success Measures

#47: Solicit stakeholder feedback to set goals and measure success.
#48: Measure HOW the team is working, not just WHAT is achieved.
#49: Review team learning regularly to be agile.
#50: Assess team effectiveness regularly.

Also by Peters and Carr

"While many leaders and coaches are well intentioned, they are frequently disappointed with their outcomes when trying to create high performing teams. *50 Tips for Terrific Teams* has brilliantly integrated the research... and translated it into practical suggestions that will absolutely help create the desired shifts. This guide is user friendly and the closest thing to having your own personal sage."

- Denise Still, MSW, RSW, PCC, CEC
Calgary Board of Education

Dr. Jacqueline Peters, PCC, CHRP is an Executive Coach, author and Organizational Consultant with over 20 years of internal and external experience improving the business performance of leaders, teams and organizations. Dr. Peters is the founder of *InnerActive Leadership Associates.*

Dr. Catherine Carr, PCC, RCC is an Executive Coach, author and Organizational Consultant with over 20 years of experience guiding individuals, teams and organizations to realize their fullest potential. Dr. Carr is the founder of *Catherine Carr and Associates.*

Jacqueline.Peters@InnerActive.ca
www.InnerActiveLeadership.ca

Dr.CatherineCarr@gmail.com
www.CatherineCarr.ca

InnerActive

www.HighPerformanceTeamCoaching.com

References and Resources for Further Reading

Ancona, D., and Bresman, H. (2007) *X-Teams: How to build teams that lead, innovate, and succeed.* Boston: Harvard Business School Press.

Anderson, M., Anderson, D., and Mayo, W. (2008) Team coaching helps a leadership team drive cultural change at caterpillar. *Global Business and Organizational Excellence*, 27(4), pp.40-50.

Barrick, M., Mount, M., and Judge, T. (2001) The FFM personality dimensions and job performance: meta-analysis of meta-analyses. *International Journal of Selection and Assessment*, 9, pp.9-30.

Blattner, J., and Bacigalupo, A. (2007) Using emotional intelligence to develop executive leadership and team and organisational development. *Consulting Psychology Journal: Practice and Research*, 59(3), pp.209-219.

Brown, S.W., and Grant, A.M. (2010) From GROW to GROUP: theoretical issues and a practical model for group coaching in organisations. *Coaching: An International Journal of Theory, Research and Practice*, 3(1), pp.30-45.

Buckingham, M., and Coffman, C. (1999). *First, break all the rules: what the world's greatest managers do differently.* New York: Simon & Schuster.

Carr, C., and Peters, J. (2012) *The experience and impact of team coaching: a dual case study.* Doctoral dissertation, Middlesex University.

Carr, C., and Peters, J. (2013) The experience and impact of team coaching: a dual case study. *International Journal Coaching Psychology Review*, 8(1). pp.80-98.

Clutterbuck, D. (2007) *Coaching the team at work.* London: Good News Press.

Corporate Leadership Council (2011). *The power of peers: building engagement capital through peer interaction* [Internet] Available from: http://greatmanager.ucsf.edu/files/CLC_The_Power_of_Peers_Building_Engagement_Capital_Through_Peer_Interaction.pdf [Accessed 31 January 2013].

Cox, E. (2012) Individual and organizational trust in a reciprocal peer coaching context. *Mentoring & Tutoring: Partnership in Learning*, 20(3), pp.427-443.

Coyne, K., and Coyne, S. (2011) *Brainsteering: a better approach to break-through ideas.* New York: Harper Collins Publishers.

Cross R., Gray. P., Cunningham. S., Showers, M., and Thomas, R.J. (2010) The Collaborative Organization: How to Make Employee Networks Really Work. *MIT Sloan Review* [Internet] Available from: http://sloanreview.mit.edu/article/the-collaborative-organization-how-to-make-employee-networks-really-work/ [Accessed 31 January, 2013].

Edmondson, A. (1999) Psychological safety and learning behavior in work teams. *Administrative Science Quarterly*, 4(2), pp.350-383.

Edmondson, A. (2012) *Teaming: how organizations learn, innovate, and compete in the knowledge economy.* San Francisco, CA: Jossey-Bass.

Felps, W., Mitchell, T., and Byington, E. (2006) How, when and why bad apples spoil the barrel: negative group members and dysfunctional groups. *An Annual Series of Analytical Essays and Critical Reviews, Research in Organizational Behavior*, 27, pp.175-222.

Ferrazzi, K. (2012) How successful virtual teams collaborate. *Harvard Business Review* [Internet] Available from: http://blogs.hbr.org/cs/2012/10/how_to_collaborate_in_a_virtua.html. [Accessed 31 January, 2013].

Fredrickson, B., and Losada, M. (2005) Positive affect and the complex dynamics of human flourishing. *American Psychologist*, 60(7), pp.678-686.

Gersick, C. (1988) Time and transition in work teams: toward a new model of group development. *Academy of Management Journal*, 31(1), pp.9-41.

Gottman, J. (1994) *What predicts divorce: the relationship between marital processes and marital outcomes.* Hillsdale, New Jersey: Lawrence Erlbaum Associates.

Gruenfeld, D., Martorana, P., and Fan, E. (2000) What do groups learn from their worldliest members? Direct and indirect influence in dynamic teams. *Organizational Behavior and Human Decision Processes*, 82, pp.45-59.

Guttman, H. (2008) *Great business teams: cracking the code for standout performance.* Hoboken, New Jersey: John Wiley and Sons.

Hackman, J.R. (1987) The design of work teams. In: J. Lorasch, ed. *Handbook of organizational behavior*. Englewood Cliffs, NJ: Prentice-Hall, pp.315-342.

Hackman, J.R. (2011) Six common misperceptions about teamwork. *Harvard Business Review*, [Internet blog]. Available from: http://blogs.hbr.org/cs/2011/06/six_common_misperceptions_abou.html [Accessed 23 June 2011].

Hackman, J.R. (2012) From causes to conditions in group research. *Journal of Organizational Behavior*, 33(3), pp.428-444.

Hackman, J.R., and O'Connor, M. (2005) *What makes for a great analytic team? Individual vs. team approaches to intelligence analysis*. Washington, DC, Intelligence Science Board, Office of the Director of Central Intelligence.

Hackman, J.R., and Wageman, R. (2005) A theory of team coaching, *Academy of Management Review*, 30(2), pp.269–287.

Haug, M. (2011) What is the relationship between coaching interventions and team effectiveness? *International Journal of Evidence Based Coaching and Mentoring*, Special Issue No.5, pp.89-101.

Hawkins, P. (2011) *Leadership team coaching: developing collective transformational leadership*. Philadelphia, PA: Kogan Page Publishers.

Johnson, S., Suriya, C., Yoon, S., Berrett, J., and La Fleur, J, (2002) Team development and group processes of virtual learning teams. *Computers & Education*, 39, pp. 379-393.

LaFasto, F., and Larson, C. (2001) *When teams work best: 6,000 team members and leaders tell what it takes to succeed*. Thousand Oaks, CA: Sage Publications.

Losada M., and Heaphy E. (2004) The role of positivity and negativity in the performance of business teams. *The American Behavioral Scientist*, 47, pp.740-765.

Losada, M. (2008) Want to flourish? Stay in the zone. *Positive Psychology Daily News 8* December, [Internet blog]. Available from: http://positivepsychologynews.com/news/marcial-losada/200812081289 [Accessed 23 June 2011].

McGrath, J., Arrow, H., and Berdahl, J. (2000) The study of groups: past, present, and future. *Personality and Social Psychology Review*, 4(1), pp.95-105.

McKenna, M., Shelton, D., and Darling, J. (2002) The impact of behavioral style assessment on organizational effectiveness: a call for action. *Leadership and Organization Development Journal*, 23(6), pp.314-322.

Meier, D. (2005) *Team coaching with the solution circle: a practical guide to solution focused team development.* Cheltenham, UK: Solutions Books.

Mesmer-Magnus, J., and DeChurch, L. (2009) Information sharing and team performance: a meta-analysis. *Journal of Applied Psychology*, 94(2), pp.535-546.

Mulec, K., and Roth, J. (2005) Action, reflection, and learning and coaching in order to enhance the performance of drug development project management teams. *R and D Management*, 35, pp.483-491.

Pate, L., and Shoblom, T. (2013) The ACES decision-making technique for increasing empathy when people don't care. *Organizing through empathy.* Routledge. Forthcoming.

Pentland, S. (2012) Science of building great teams. *Harvard Business Review*, 90(4), pp.60-70.

Peters, J. (2013) *High performance team effectiveness assessment.* Calgary, Alberta, Canada: InnerActive Leadership Associates Inc. Forthcoming.

Peters, J., and Carr, C. (2013) *High performance team coaching: a comprehensive system for leaders and coaches.* Calgary, Alberta, Canada: InnerActive Leadership Associates Inc.

Potter, R., and Balthazard, P. (2002) Understanding human interaction and performance in the virtual team. *Journal of Information Technology Theory and Application* (JITTA), 4(1).

Reilly, R., Lynn G., and Aronson H. (2002) The role of personality in new product development team performance. *Journal of Engineering Technology Management*, 19, pp.39-58.

Rico, R., de la Hera, C, and Tabernero, C. (2011) Work team effectiveness: a review of research from the last decade (1999-2009). *Psychology in Spain*, 15(1), pp.57-79.

Singer, B. (2004) *The ABC's of building a business team that wins: the invisible code of honor that takes ordinary people and turns them into a championship team*. New York: Warner Books.

Stock, R. (2004) Drivers of team performance: what do we know and what have we still to learn? *Schmalenbach Business Review*, 56, pp.274-306.

Switzler, A. (2009) *Crucial Skills*. [Internet] Available from: http://www.crucialskills.com/2009/12/rebuilding-trust-after-layoffs/. [Accessed 11 February 2013].

Tekleab, A., Quigley, N., and Tesluk, P. (2009) A longitudinal study of team conflict, conflict management, cohesion, and team effectiveness. *Group and Organization Management*, 34, pp.170-205.

Wageman, R., Hackman, J.R., and Lehman, E. (2005) Team diagnostic survey: development of an instrument. *Journal of Applied Behavioral Science*, 41, pp.373-398.

Wageman, R., Nunes, D., Burruss, J., and Hackman, J.R. (2008) *Senior leadership teams: what it takes to make them great*. Boston, Harvard Business School Publishing Corporation.

Wageman, R., Fisher, C., and Hackman, J.R. (2009) Leading teams when the timing is right: finding the best moments to act. *Organizational Dynamics*, 38(3), pp.192-203.

Watson Wyatt Work Study (2008) *Driving business results through continuous engagement* (2008/2009 WorkUSA Survey Report). USA: Watson Wyatt Worldwide.

Woolley, A., Gerbasi, M., Chabris, C., Kosslyn, S., and Hackman, J.R. (2008) Bringing in the experts: how team composition and collaborative planning jointly shape analytic effectiveness. *Small Group Research*, 39, pp.352-371.

Woolley, A.W., Chabris, C.F., Pentland, A., Hashmi, N., and Malone, T.W. (2010) *Evidence for a collective intelligence factor in the performance of human groups.* [Internet] Available from:
http://www.sciencemag.org/search?author1=Christopher+F.+Chabris&sortspec=date&submit=Submit Science, published online 30 September 2010. pp.686-688.
[Accessed January 10, 2013].

Woolley, A.W., and Malone, T.W. (2011) Defend your research: what makes a team smarter? More women. *Harvard Business Review*, 89(6), pp.32-33.

About the Authors

Jacqueline Peters, B.Sc., M.Ed., DProf, PCC, CHRP

Executive coach and team and leadership specialist Dr. Jacqueline Peters has over 20 years of experience coaching leaders, executives, and teams to achieve higher performance. Jacqueline's clients say that her unique mix of practical corporate experience and doctoral level knowledge of leadership, coaching, and team effectiveness helps them achieve and exceed their personal and team productivity goals. She and Dr. Catherine Carr co-developed the High Performance Team Coaching System, a robust approach developed for leaders and coaches that is grounded in the research and proven practices that build team effectiveness.

Prior to coaching and facilitating leadership teams through her own company, Jacqueline spent many years working as a senior leader focused on management and leadership development in large corporations. Jacqueline is a professional member of the Canadian Association of Professional Speakers (CAPS), and a professional certified coach (PCC) with the International Coaching Federation (ICF). She has a Doctorate (DProf) in Leadership Development and Coaching from Middlesex University (UK), specializing in team coaching. The dissertation that she co-authored with Catherine Carr was awarded the Ken Goulding award for the most outstanding professional doctorate at Middlesex University in 2012.

Catherine Carr, B.Sc., M.Ed., DProf, PCC, RCC

Catherine has 20 years of experience in leadership development, group and team coaching, coach training and supervision, and program facilitation. She offers evidence-based approaches to coaching and organizational development. Catherine is known for her warmth and confidence building approach and draws on her extensive background in counseling psychology. She supports and motivates leaders and teams to imagine their ideal and make it real.

In 2011 Catherine helped design and launch the British Columbia Public Service Agency's innovative team coaching service, which is embarking on team coaching services for potentially 26,000 staff. Her current work includes developing coaching culture initiatives for organizations, of which team coaching is an essential component. Catherine is a professional certified coach (PCC) with the International Coaching Federation (ICF). She has a Doctorate (DProf) in Leadership Development and Executive Coaching from Middlesex University (UK), specializing in team coaching. She co-developed the High Performance Team Coaching system underlying this book with Dr. Jacqueline Peters. The dissertation that she co-authored with Jacqueline Peters was awarded the Ken Goulding Award for the most outstanding professional doctorate at Middlesex University in 2012.

CPSIA information can be obtained
at www.ICGtesting.com
Printed in the USA
LVOW07s0759231017

553427LV00013B/627/P

9 781460 225691